CHRISTMAS CAROLS FOR TWO

Arrangements by Mark Phillips

ISBN 978-1-5400-2915-7

Copyright © 2018 by HAL LEONARD LLC
International Copyright Secured   All Rights Reserved

Contact Us:
Hal Leonard
7777 West Bluemound Road
Milwaukee, WI 53213
Email: info@halleonard.com

In Europe contact:
Hal Leonard Europe Limited
Distribution Centre, Newmarket Road
Bury St Edmunds, Suffolk, IP33 3YB
Email: info@halleonardeurope.com

In Australia contact:
Hal Leonard Australia Pty. Ltd.
4 Lentara Court
Cheltenham, Victoria, 3192 Australia
Email: info@halleonard.com.au

CONTENTS

ANGELS WE HAVE HEARD ON HIGH

FLUTES

Traditional French Carol

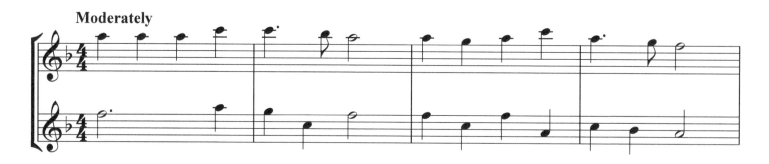

AWAY IN A MANGER

FLUTES

Music by James R. Murray

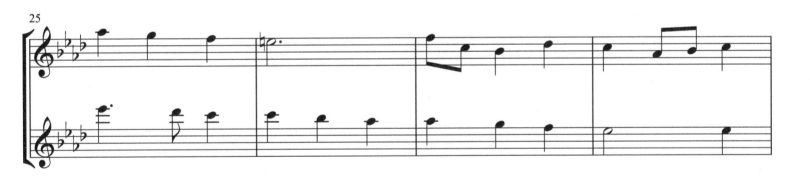

BRING A TORCH, JEANNETTE, ISABELLA

FLUTES

17th Century French Provençal Carol

Moderately slow, in 1

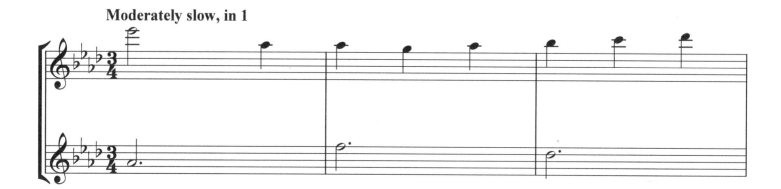

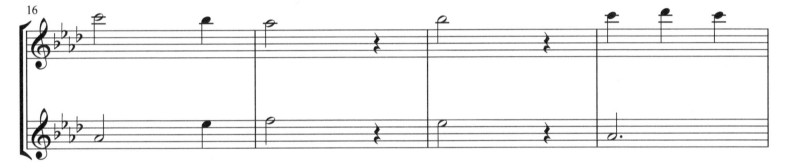

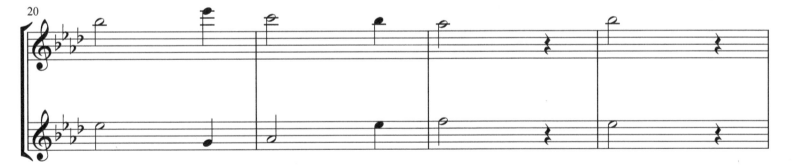

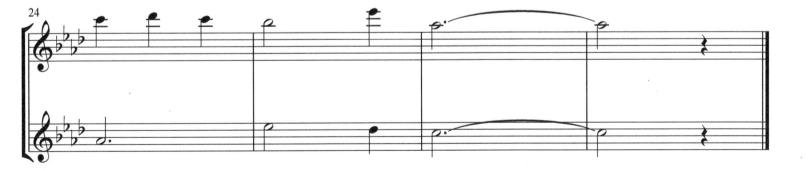

DECK THE HALL

FLUTES

Traditional Welsh Carol

Brightly

THE FIRST NOEL

FLUTES

17th Century English Carol
Music from W. Sandys' *Christmas Carols*

Moderately

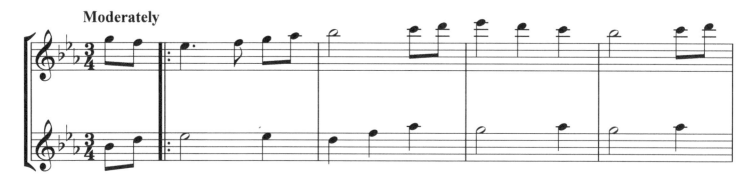

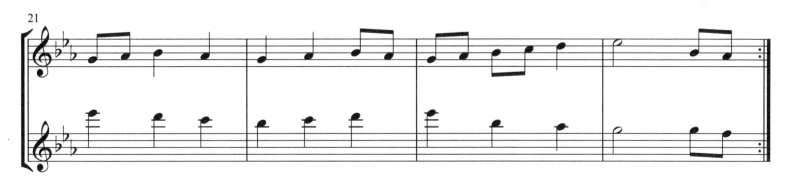

GO, TELL IT ON THE MOUNTAIN

FLUTES

African-American Spiritual

GOD REST YE MERRY, GENTLEMEN

FLUTES

Traditional English Carol

Moderately fast

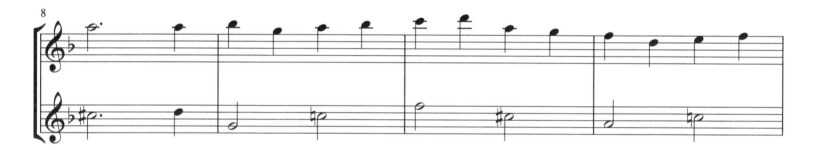

HARK! THE HERALD ANGELS SING

FLUTES

Music by Felix Mendelssohn-Bartholdy
Arranged by William H. Cummings

Brightly

IT CAME UPON THE MIDNIGHT CLEAR

FLUTES

Music by Richard Storrs Willis

Moderately slow, in 2

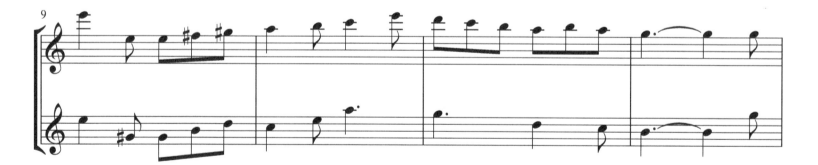

JINGLE BELLS

FLUTES

Words and Music by J. Pierpont

Brightly, in 2

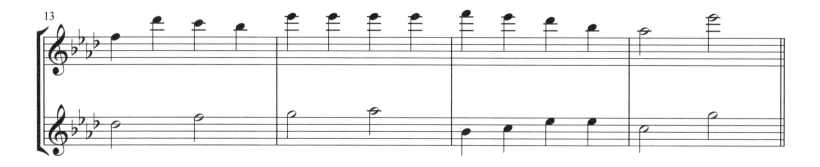

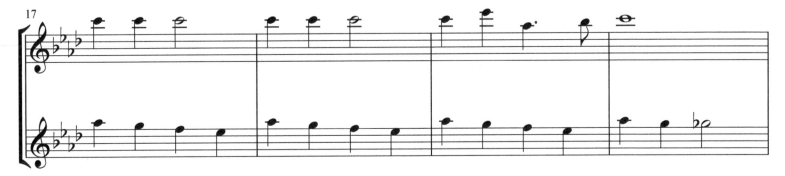

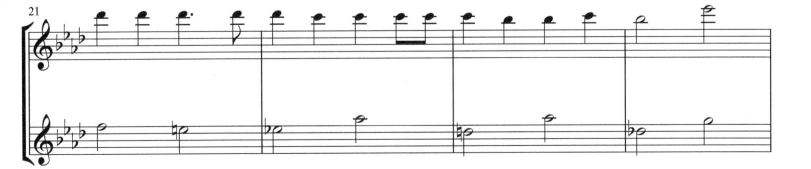

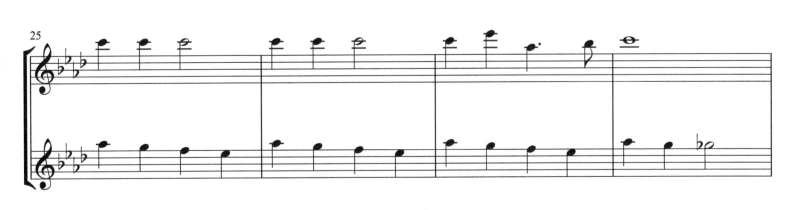

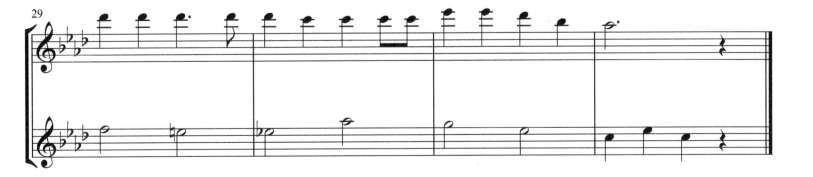

JOLLY OLD ST. NICHOLAS

FLUTES

Traditional 19th Century American Carol

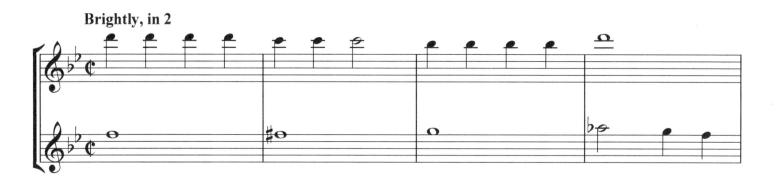

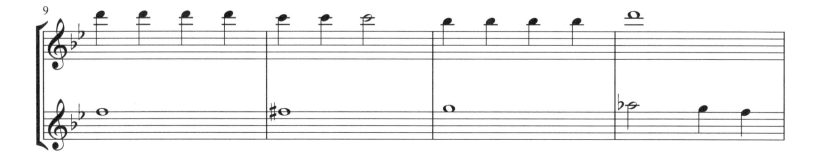

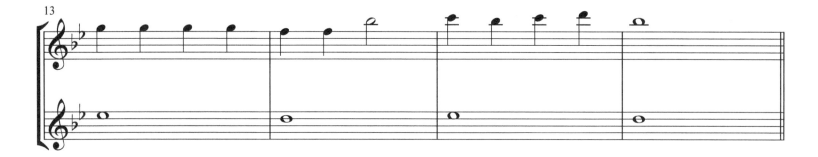

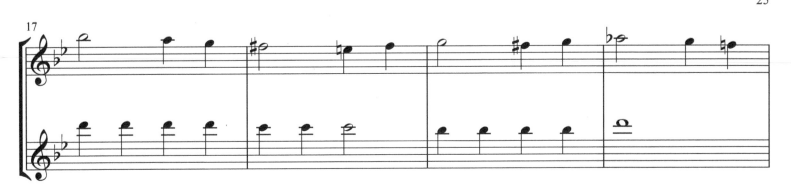

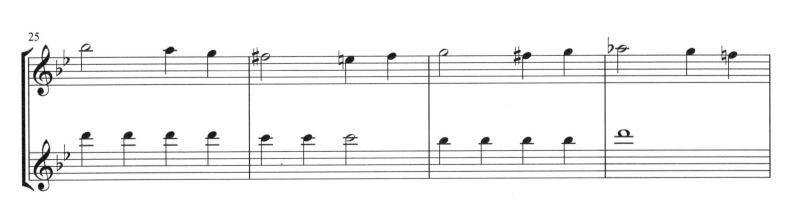

JOY TO THE WORLD

FLUTES

Music by George Frideric Handel
Adapted by Lowell Mason

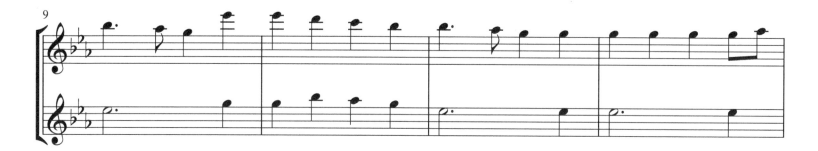

O CHRISTMAS TREE

FLUTES

Traditional German Carol

Moderately

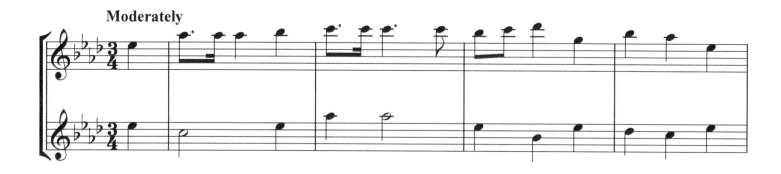

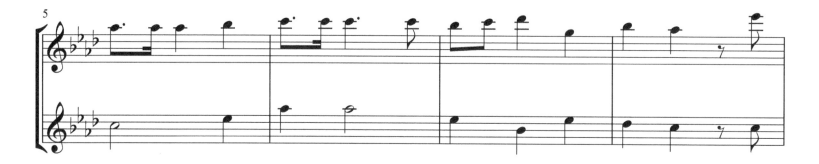

O COME, ALL YE FAITHFUL

FLUTES

Music by John Francis Wade

Moderately

O COME, O COME, EMMANUEL

FLUTES

15th Century French Melody
Adapted by Thomas Helmore

Moderately slow, in 2

O HOLY NIGHT

FLUTES

Music by Adolphe Adam

Moderately slow, in 2

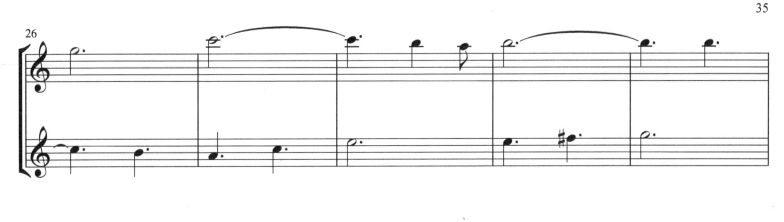

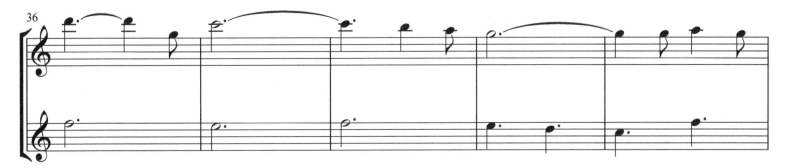

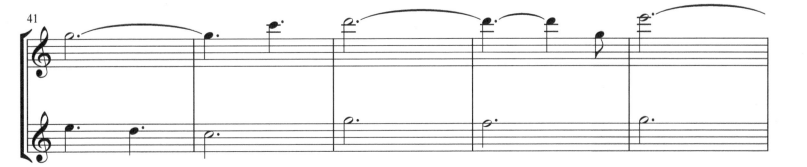

O LITTLE TOWN OF BETHLEHEM

FLUTES

Music by Lewis H. Redner

SILENT NIGHT

FLUTES

Music by Franz X. Gruber

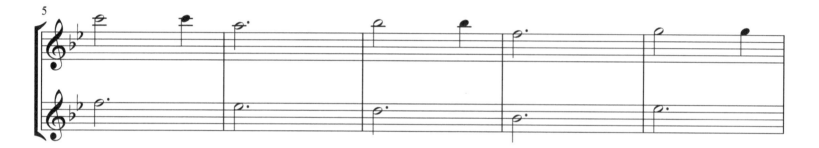

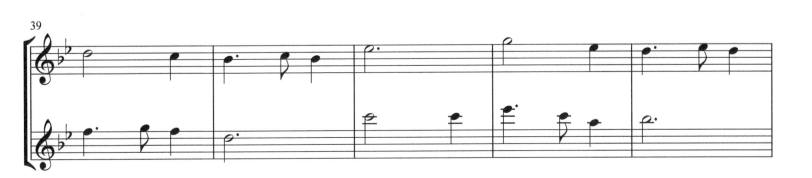

STILL, STILL, STILL

FLUTES

Salzburg Melody, c.1819

Moderately slow

WE THREE KINGS OF ORIENT ARE

FLUTES

Words and Music by John H. Hopkins, Jr.

WE WISH YOU A MERRY CHRISTMAS

FLUTES

Traditional English Folksong

WHAT CHILD IS THIS?

FLUTES

16th Century English Melody

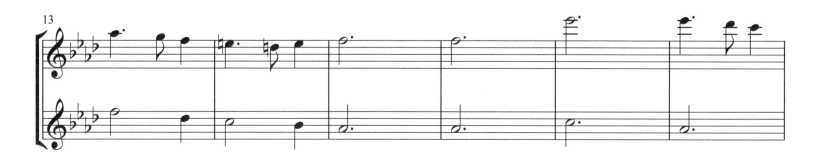

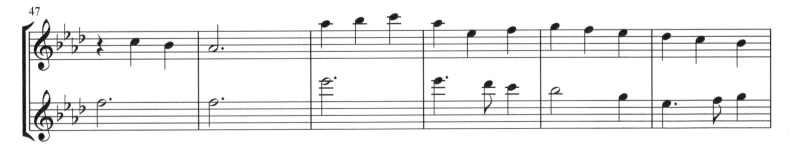